Dedicated to All of My Amazing Family

My beautiful daughters Grace Smith and Akia Moore,
and my granddaughter Anaria, you are my life.
My mom Geraldine Grant, Gwen Williams, my sister,
Kneshia Keitt (Todd), my nieces Mia, Tajh, Kensleigh,
Kameron, and Ieshia Grant, you are the reasons
why I smile.

Book Credits:

Author, Angie Smith

Cover Photo,

Graphic Designer, Excel Publishings

Publisher, J2P Global Institute

Contact Info:
grantsmithangie@yahoo.com

Acknowledgement:

I would like to acknowledge and thank God for allowing me to be able to do this. Isn't it wonderful that God knows us. Mercy. If it had not been for him speaking into my hearing, this book would not have been possible.

I would also like to acknowledge Alexander ``AL" Smith, my husband. His death was a shock, a surprise, unreal. You know how you know things are going to happen, but you never expect them to? Well, I know we all will die one day, but I never expected him to. The last words I heard from him were "It is well. It is well". I thank God for those words because I use them daily when life happens. When things come against me or I am having a moment. Each time I use those words they remind me of Al and it causes me to smile. So, you see you can find a smile in the midst of pain and adversity.

The Promises of God are yes and Amen. No one or nothing can change that. It is his word so whatever he promises you he will make good on it. Wait on him. Trust him. His promises shall come to pass.

"For no matter how many promises God has made, they are "Yes" in Christ. And so through him the "Amen" is spoken by us to the glory of God." 2 Corinthians 1:20 NIV

Today's Prayer

Thank you Father for another day. Thank you for loving and Blessing me. Thank you Father for you are my peace and strength. When chaos is happening all around me , you give me peace, you strengthen me. Father help me to not get distracted. Help me to stay focus on you.

"You will keep in perfect peace those whose minds are steadfast, because they trust in you" Isaiah 26:3 NIV

"He gives strength to the weary and increases the power of the weak" Isaiah 40:29 NIV

In Jesus Name Amen
Safe in his arms
Journey to please God
It is well. It is well.

Today's Prayer

Good morning Father. Thank you for another wonderful day. Thank you for early rising and the ability to walk, talk, think, and dress myself. Thank you Father that you are with me and no matter happens today we will work through it together. Thank you for peace through every situation. Thank you Father that today will be a great day. Unanswered prayers will be answered. Difficult situations will be made easy. Forgiveness will take place. Families will be reunited. Those who haven't spoken to each other in a while will have a conversation. Grudges will be forgiven. Relationships will be restored. Love will replace hate. Joy will replace sadness. Today Father will be a great day.

In Jesus Name Amen
I am Safe in his arms
Journey to please God
It is well. It is well.

Today's Prayer

Thank you Father for another wonderful day. I am waking to
new mercies, and new opportunities. Thank you. Thank you
that I am able to leave yesterday in the past and that I don't
have to give thought for tomorrow for you have already
taken care of them both. You knew the events of yesterday,
today and tomorrow before they would happen and you had
already prepared ways of escape for those temptations that
would come to distract and take me off focus. Thank you
Father that I be wise enough to take your way of escape, to
follow the path that you have set for me. Father I pray peace
and Blessings over the land. I pray our minds be the minds of
that which is in Christ Jesus. Help us with our thoughts.
Renew our minds, our thoughts afresh daily, hourly, by the
minute. Help us Father to stay in your will.

In Jesus Name Amen
I am safe in his arms
Journey to please God
It is well. It is well.

Today's Prayer

Thank you Father for another day and another opportunity to make a difference in the lives of the people I come in contact with. I pray today Father we glorify you with our words and our actions. I pray you are pleased with what we do and say. Today Father I ask that you cover and keep us; Lead and direct us in the way you would have us to go. I pray Father that you would protect us from all hurt harm and danger. Keep us under your wings. Help us Father to seek you, and follow your direction.

In Jesus Name Amen
Safe in his arms
Journey to please God
It is well. It is well.

Today's Prayer

Thank you Father for another day. Thank you for early rising and for having good health and strength. As I pray Father I thank you for your protection and your angels that stand guard around us. I pray for families that are experiencing the loss of a loved one. I pray peace and comfort for them. I pray that you will fill them with your joy. I pray Father for those that feel they have no other choice but to cause harm to others. I pray you give them clarity, knowledge, and understanding, so that they can make the right/better decisions. I pray for the world. Father let your spirit fall fresh on us all. Help us to live better, to do better. Help us to love our neighbors as we love our selves. Help us to see each other as you see us. Help us Father. Help us.

In Jesus Name Amen
Safe in his arms
Journey to please God
It is well. It is well.

Today's Prayer

Good morning Father. Thank you for another day. Thank you for another opportunity to praise, worship and thank you for the many Blessings you have bestowed upon me. Today Father I pray that miracles happen. I pray that situations be changed. I pray that minds be changed and that hope be restored. Today Father I pray that your sons and daughters will experience you like never before. I pray that you move on their behalf in such a way that they will know that it was nobody but you. I pray Father that relationships with you be strengthen. I pray Father that you lift the wait of depression and suicidal thoughts. I pray Father that you remove the feelings of hopelessness and defeat. I pray Father that you create in us all a clean/ pure heart and renew a right spirit within us all. Than you Father. Thank you.

In Jesus Name Amen
Safe in his arms
Journey to please God
It is well. It is well.

Today's Prayer

Good morning Father. Thank you for another day. Thank you for another opportunity to praise, worship and thank you for the many Blessings you have bestowed upon me. Today Father I pray that miracles happen. I pray that situations be changed. I pray that minds be changed and that hope be restored. Today Father I pray that your sons and daughters will experience you like never before. I pray that you move on their behalf in such a way that they will know that it was nobody but you. I pray Father that relationships with you be strengthen. I pray Father that you lift the wait of depression and suicidal thoughts. I pray Father that you remove the feelings of hopelessness and defeat. I pray Father that you create in us all a clean/ pure heart and renew a right spirit within us all. Than you Father. Thank you.

In Jesus Name Amen
Safe in his arms
Journey to please God
It is well. It is well.

Today's Prayer

Good morning Father. Thank you for waking me to the beginning
of another wonderful day. Thank you Father that today will be all
that you created it to be. We bind every attempt of satan to distract
us, to get us off track and to cause us to act out of character. We
thank you Father that we will walk in the steps that you have
planned for us and that we will follow your guidance. We thank
you Father that no weapon formed against us shall prosper and
every attack of satan is defeated. We Thank you Father that we are
overcomers, we are conquers. There is nothing that we can't do
with Jesus who strengthens us and you Father who fights for us.
Today we walk in victory. Every plan that was sent out to rob, kill,
and destroy us has been defeated. We thank you Father.

In Jesus Name, Amen
Safe in his arms
Journey to please God
It is well. It is well.

Today's Prayer

Good morning Father. Thank you for another amazing day. Thank you for another early rising and being able to acknowledge who you are and all that you have done and continue to do for me. It is truly a Blessing to be your child. On today Father I thank you for providing ways for those of us who are having difficulty making ends meet. I pray for those who are experiencing sickness in the mind and body. I pray they will experience your word which says according to your riches in glory you will supply all their needs. I pray Father that they will experience your word that says you are the God that healeth thee: that all sickness is not unto death; that by your stripes they are healed. I pray Father they know if your word says it then it is true, that they can trust your word. I pray Father that they don't allow their circumstances to cloud who you are and what you can do. Let them know Father that in you they are safe and protected. That they are healed and delivered.

In Jesus Name, Amen
Safe in his arms
Journey to please God
It is well. It is well.

Today's Prayer

Good morning Father. Thank you for another amazing day. Thank you for early rising and your peace. Thank you Father for the joy that came with this morning. Thank you for making it through yesterday and victory on today. Thank you Father that every weapon that formed for me today has already been defeated. Father I pray for those with heavy hearts, those who feel defeated and don't know which way to go. Remind them of your word which says for them to lean not on their own understanding but to acknowledge you and you will direct their path. Help them find their way and to stay on your path. Renew in them a clean heart and sustain them, keep them Father. Don't let them get weary. Let them Know they can cast their cares on you, that you are a burden bearer, a lifter of heads and a problem solver.

In Jesus Name, Amen
Safe in his arms
Journey to please God
It is well. It is well.

"The LORD guides people in the way they should go and protects those who please him. If they fall, they will not stay down, because the LORD will help them up."
Psalms 37:23-24 GNB

"If you wander off the road to the right or the left, you will hear his voice behind you saying, "Here is the road. Follow it."" Isaiah 30:21 GNB

Today's Prayer

Good morning Father. Thank you for another wonderful day. Thank you for life and the things that we take for granted. We thank you for what we call the big things but we often fail to thank for the "little" things. Forgive us Father. We thank you. We thank you for the ability to walk without assistance, to blink our eyes, lift our hands, turn from side to side. Father, thank you. We go about our daily task and forget sometimes to say thank you. Thank you that we have a job, a place to stay, a car to drive,food to eat. Thank you. Thank you for lights, clothes, running water to drink and wash with. Father, I don't take these things for granted. I am thankful because I know some don't have these things. I also know that if not for you, it could have been me. Father I am thankful, I am grateful for all that you do for me. I am grateful that your love is the same for all and what you do for one you do for others. Touch the heart of those that are facing challenges, that don't have all they need, want ,or desire and let them know that you are a provider of needs, a giver of wants and desires. Touch them Father and help them to know that you are working things for their good, that you are opening doors for their needs to be met. Father give them the strength to hold on and not quit before they reap their harvest.

In Jesus Name, Amen
Safe in his arms
Journey to please God
It is well. It is well.

Today's Prayer

Good morning Father. Thank you for another amazing day.
Thank you for early rising and having the ability to think,
walk , and talk. Thank you for always being with me. Thank
you for answered prayers. Whether it is what I want, need, or
desire, you always give me what is best for me. Thank you
for creating and knowing me. Thank you for planning and
making ways for me. I pray Father that all your children are
open to have a relationship with, worship, praise, and receive
from you. Thank you Father that you are not like me, you
don't get frustrated, aggravated and quit, or give up on your
children. Thank you that you give chance after chance and
unconditional love. Thank you Father, for your desire and
will to prosper us and not harm us, to give us a future filled
with hope. Thank you Father. Thank you.

In Jesus Name, Amen
Safe in his arms
Journey to please God
It is well. It is well.

Today's Prayer

Good morning Father. Thank you for another wonderful day. Thank you for early rising and being able to know who you are and who I am. Thank you for good health and strength. As I pray Father, I thank you that troubles, trials, don't last always, and that you work all things for our good. I thank you that joy does come, change does happen. I thank you Father that no matter what it looks or feel like, I am coming out victorious, purified, clean and renewed. I am so glad you Father have the final say, that you have the ending to my situation. Help me Father to hold on, to make it until my change comes. Help me to not give up before you work it out. Father Thank you for the peace, strength and ability to hold on, to wait on you through the turbulences. Thank you for allowing me to to focus on you and your goodness, power and ability.

In Jesus Name, Amen
Safe in his arms
Journey to please God
It is well. It is well.

A change is gonna come. Oh yes it will.
(Sam Cooke)
Wait on it

Today's Prayer

Thank you Father for another wonderful day. Thank you for the new mercies that it brings. Thank you Father that I am able to call on your name. I thank you that I am able to do the things that you have for me to do and to have the things that you have for me on this day. Thank you Father that I make plans and they may or may not happen but your plans for me are established by you and I can be sure that they will happen. Thank you Father that I live and walk in your plans. As I pray Father help those who don't know what your plan is for them. Help those that are seeking to know who they are and what their purpose is. Help them to seek you their creator for direction. Let them know Father that you know the plans you have for them and that your plans are to prosper them (cause them to succeed, thrive, grow), to give them hope and a future, to not harm them. Help them to trust your plan. Take away their doubt, uncertainty, and fear.

In Jesus Name, Amen
Safe in his arms
Journey to please God
It is well. It is well.

Today's Prayer

Good morning Father. Thank you for another wonderful day.
Thank you for your Goodness, Grace, Mercy and Favor.
Thank you Father for you are our refuge, and our strong
tower. There is no problem or situation that you can't handle.
As I pray Father, I ask that you wrap your arms around your
children. There are some that are needing to feel your touch,
some that need to be reminded of your power, and some that
just need to know that you are still there with them. Father I
ask in the name of Jesus that you touch, set free, and deliver
your people from the traps, tricks, schemes, plots of Satan,
and the strongholds that are weighing us down. Thank you
Father, Thank you for allowing ways of escape from all of
these things and for the ability to to endure them until our
change come. Help us to live the life of abundance that Jesus
came for us to live. Help us to live in overflow of your grace,
goodness, mercy, and favor.

In Jesus Name, Amen
Safe in his arms
Journey to please God
It is well. It is well.

*"The thief cometh not, but for to steal, and to kill, and to
destroy: I am come that they might have life, and that they
might have it more abundantly"*   John 10:10

Today's Prayer

Good morning Father. Thank you for another beautiful day.
Thank you for all that today will bring. Thank you for
working everything for my good. Thank you that every good
and perfect gift comes from you. Thank you, Father, that
even the strong get tired and weary but they don't quit. They
don't give up. Instead, Father, they look to you and you
renew their strength, you give them hope. Thank you that our
circumstances don't predict who we are or where we will
end up. Thank you, Father, that regardless of our situation
you have the final say. You Father can take what looks
hopeless and dead and give life to it. Thank you for speaking
life to our circumstances and bringing hope to our situations.

In Jesus Name, Amen
Safe in his arms
Journey to please God
It is well. It is well.

Today's Prayer

Good morning Father. Thank you for another wonderful day.
Thank you that I am able to call on your name and that you
hear me. Thank you for safety from seen and unseen
dangers. Thank you for always watching over me. Even in
the times when I feel alone I know that you are there. Father
I pray that you would Forgive us for our sins against you,
that you would Forgive us for our disobedience against you.
I pray Father that you would touch us. Touch our heart,
mind, soul, and spirit. Renew in us a right spirit. Create in us
a clean heart. Revive us Father. Let your anointing fall fresh
on us. Blow a wind of repentance, healing and deliverance
over us. Let your word fall fresh and deep within us.
Help us to grow in you. Help us to walk in your will and
your way. Help us Father Help us.

In Jesus Name, Amen
Safe in his arms
Journey to please God
It is well. It is well.

Today's Prayer

Good morning Father. Thank you for another beautiful day and another week. You brought me through. You kept me through every situation that came my way. You kept my mind and body. I pray Father that you will help those that are battling in their minds and fighting sickness in their bodies. Show them the life of your living word which says you will keep in perfect peace those whose minds are stayed on you. Help them to focus on you so they can experience your perfect peace. Show them your living word that says because of our transgressions he was wounded and because of our iniquities he was bruised, the chastisement for our peace was upon him and by his stripes we are healed. Show them your word that says you are the God that heals. Manifest your healing in them Father. Thank you, Father, for peace and healing.

In Jesus Name, Amen
Safe in his arms
Journey to please God
It is well. It is well.

Today's Prayer

Good morning Father. Thank you for another great night's rest and early rising . Thank you for standing guard over our lives. Thank you for watching over the word you have spoken over our lives to ensure that they become reality. As we begin our day Father we thank you for world peace and unity. We thank you Father that even the unjust just like the just have to bow down when you speak. Thank you Father that you have the power to change any situation at any time. I pray that all that are experiencing difficulties know that you can change their circumstances. I pray they don't get weary and they continue to serve you. I pray that they hold on to your word. I pray Father that they are able to experience your goodness while here in the land of the living.

In Jesus Name, Amen
Safe in his arms
Journey to please God
It is well. It is well.

Today's Prayer

Good morning Father. Thank you for another wonderful day.
Thank you for your peace that surpasses all understanding.
Thank you for your never ending joy. Thank you for your
Holy Spirit that dwells within us. Thank you for your
direction, guidance, protection and correction. Thank you
Father that you know what I need and you provide it for me.
I pray Father that your peace covers the world on today. I
pray for peace throughout the land. I pray that every plan
that satan has set for today be destroyed and all evil thoughts
be turned into shouts of joy and happiness. On this day
Father let your anointing fall fresh on all of us, let your spirit
touch our hearts and our minds. Let us think and act
according to your will and your plans. Let us move self out
of the way. Thank you, Father, that your will shall be done
on earth as it is done in heaven.

In Jesus Name, Amen
Safe in his arms
Journey to please God
It is well. It is well.

Today's Prayer

Good morning Father. Thank you for another wonderful day. Each morning that I open my eyes to another day, I am absolutely grateful. I thank you that with each new morning comes new mercies. Everyday comes with new opportunities to get things right with you, to please you, and to live according to your will. Thank you Father for how you watch over your children, how you provide for us, how you keep us. Thank you for not allowing our foolishness and disobedience to cause you to turn your back on us. Thank you for seeing beyond our physical presentation and seeing who you created us to be. Thank you for loving us in spite of ourselves. Help us Father to please you and not bring shame to you. Help us not to disappoint you, but instead to live pleasing and acceptable in your sight. Forgive us Father for our sins, known and unknown.

In Jesus Name, Amen
Safe in his arms
Journey to please God
It is well. It is well.

Today's Prayer

Good morning Father. Thank you for another wonderful day. You have given me Another opportunity to become closer to you and to walk in your plans for me. Thank you Father for the desire, thirst and hunger to be more like you. I pray Father that today will be a day of forgiveness for those who are struggling with unforgiveness. I pray Father that today will be a day of unity for families who have been divided. Father, I pray for a positive resolution for those who are deciding which way to go in their relationship with you. Help them Father to see you for all that you are. Open their eyes to your love, goodness, and faithfulness to them.

In Jesus Name, Amen
Safe in his arms
Journey to please God
It is well. It is well.

Today's Prayer

Good morning Father. Thank you for another wonderful rising and awesome day. Thanking you today for the many Blessings that I have experienced because of your love, mercy and grace. I am not always worthy, don't always do right by you, but you Father never fail me. You always come through for me, you are always there, and for that Father I am grateful. Today Father as we go through our day, I ask that you speak to the hearts and minds of those who still don't understand and walk in your plan for their lives. I pray that you open their awareness to all that you have for them. I pray that they find themselves walking along your path for them. Help them to see your goodness and love for them. Help them to understand that that thing that happened to them was not your doing but that it was because of you that they made it through it. Tear down the wall Father so that they can see and experience your love. Cover them Father, keep them, show them the way, your way.

In Jesus Name, Amen
Safe in your arms
It is well. It is well.

Today's Prayer

Good morning Father. Thank you for another wonderful day. We have made it to see the passing of another week. Some Father didn't make it. We mourn for them and their families. We pray for comfort and strength to their loved ones. Thank you Father for being a fence around us. Thank you for being our sunshine in the midst of our sorrows. Thank you for lifting our bowed down heads. Father You never promised sunshine every day, but your word does say joy comes with morning, suffering won't last forever, that you will deliver us from our troubles, that in all things we are more than conquerors, that through Christ Jesus we have the victory, so today Father we thank you for our being conquerors, our joy, our deliverance, our victory and we thank you that all that we encounter, all that we go through, it is working for our good. It's working. It's working.

In Jesus Name, Amen
Safe in his arms
Journey to please God
It is well. It is well.

Today's Prayer

Good morning Father. Thank you for another wonderful day. Thank you for your joy and strength. As I start this new day that you have allowed me to be a part of, I thank you that your plans for me will manifest on today. I thank you for the new mercies that you have set aside just for me. I thank you Father that you don't get my prayers, needs, desires confused with any one else's. I thank you that what you have for me is for me. Father I thank you for those who have been praying and seeking you for direction. I pray Father that they don't give up and that they wait on you. I pray that their faith fail not. Let them know Father that you have heard their prayers and you see their situations. Remind them Father, that their time is not your time; that you always show up; that when you come in the mist of their situation, it is always the right time. Father give them strength to hold on, to wait on you.

In Jesus Name, Amen
Safe in his arms
Journey to please God
It is well. It is well.

"When the righteous cry for help, the Lord hears and delivers them out of all their troubles" Psalm 34:17 ESV

"He fulfills the desire of those who fear him; he also hears their cry and saves them" Psalm 145:19 ESV

Today's Prayer

Thank you Father for another day. Thank you for abundant life, and your strength. In all that you do for me, thank you does not relay how grateful I am that you made a choice to love me. In spite of all my flaws, mess ups and imperfections you still love me. I pray Father that you would help those that walk around looking like they have it together but are dealing with hurts, disappointments, unforgiveness, and sadness on the inside. I pray Father that they know that they can lean on you. That they can cast their cares on you. I pray Father that their inside is well, that it is just as put together as their outside appearance. Help them to unload, release their hurts, disappointments, unforgiveness, and sadness. Let their smile be real, give them your everlasting joy. Let their happiness be sincere.

In Jesus Name, Amen
Safe in his arms
Journey to please God
It is well. It is well.

Today's Prayer

Thank you Father for another day. Thank you for early rising and a fresh start to a new day. Thank you for peace of mind. Thank you for caring for me enough to allow me to be able to cast my cares, my burdens, and my problems on you. Today Father I ask a special Blessing for those that are experiencing depression. I pray Father that you would blow a fresh wind on them and help them to know that they do not have to face their problems alone. Help them Father to understand that you are there and that you can and will work out any situation that is holding them in bondage. Let them know Father the battles they face can be defeated. Help them see that they can find joy in you. Thank you Father for releasing them of their fears, worries, doubts and anxieties.

In Jesus Name, Amen
Safe in his arms
Journey to please God
It is well. It is well.

Today's Prayer

Thank you, Father, for another early rising and wonderful day. I am rejoicing because I have another opportunity to get closer to you. Thank you for the new mercies that you have given me for this day. Thank you that I rise with a desire to serve and please you. Thank you, Father, that I am able to call on your name with assurance that you hear me and that you will answer me. Thank you, Father, that I can depend on you to do what is best for me. Today I pray that you would touch and reunite families that are broken. I pray that you would cause them to forgive and forget the things that have caused divisiveness in their lives. Bring them back together Father.

In Jesus Name, Amen
Safe in his arms
Journey to please God
It is well. It is well.

Today's Prayer

Thank you Father for another wonderful day. Thank you for your wisdom and knowledge. Thank you for your plans for my life. Thank you for faith and trust in you and your word. I pray Father that you would Help us to stay in your will and to not get discouraged by what we see or feel. Help us to know that regardless of what is happening around us your desire for our lives is to have life and to have in abundance. Help us Father to stay focused and to hold on to your promises. Thank you Father that you will supply all our needs. Father, your word says that we are victorious, we are overcomers, I trust your word, I believe your word and I expect to overcome those things that are obstacles in my path. I expect to be victorious over all that is a hindrance to my living the life that you have for me.

In Jesus Name, Amen
Safe in his arms
Journey to please God
It is well. It is well.

Today's Prayer

Thank you, Father, for another day. Thank you for health and strength. Father this has been a tough year for many. Lives have been changed like never before. I pray your peace and strength to those who are dealing with the loss of a loved one and for those affected by the pandemic. Help them to make it through these difficult times. Give them your peace. Father allow your healing power to consume their bodies. Don't allow fear, worry, and doubt to cause them to question who you are and what you can do. Help them Father to have trust, faith in you. Show them your power, grace and mercy. Shine your light on their situations and give them joy in spite of their circumstances.

In Jesus Name, Amen
Safe in his arms
Journey to please God
It is well. It is well.

Today's Prayer

Thank you, Father, for another wonderful day. Thank you for another opportunity to give you glory, honor and praise for always being there for me. You Father are my ever-present help in times of trouble, my sunshine in the rain. Today Father I pray for unity in families. I pray that all grudges and differences be worked out and forgiven. I pray that families come together to love, laugh and enjoy each other. Father open doors for forgiveness and unity.

In Jesus Name, Amen
Safe in his arms
Journey to please God
It is well. It is well.

Today's Prayer

Thank you Father for another wonderful day. Thank you that I am still here, still able to acknowledge your presence in my life. Thank you Father for your goodness, and your mighty power in my life. Today Father I pray that you give direction and hope to those who have lost their way, to those that may have gotten off of the path you have for them. I pray for those that are fighting to make it through problems that have come in their lives. I pray for those that don't know what to do and are feeling overwhelmed. Touch them Father. Remind them of who you are. Show them your power and strength. Show them the way. Father Guide them, lead them to your will, your path for them. Give them strength to keep pushing their way through. Remind them that quitting is not an option. Remind them that victory is at the end of their fight, struggle, disappointment, sickness.

I decree and declare that they shall have victory in Jesus name.

In Jesus Name, Amen
Safe in his arms
Journey to please God
It is well. It is well.

Today's Prayer

Thank you, Father, for another wonderful day. Thank you for the early rise and the use of my eyes, ears, mind and limbs. Thank you, Father, for the power of prayer and being able to call on your name. Thank you, Father, that you hear us when we pray. Today Father I pray for total and complete healing for those who are sick physically, emotionally, and spiritually. I pray Father you release them from all infirmities in their bodies; that you cleanse them from any impurities and that you cover them with the blood of Jesus. Cleanse us all Father. Renew, Restore, and Revive us all.

In Jesus Name, Amen
Safe in his arms
Journey to please God
It is well. It is well.

Today's Prayer

Thank you, Father, for another great day. Thank you for another opportunity to praise you and give you glory. Thank you that I am able to know that you are a true and living God, that I am able to experience your goodness. Today Father I pray for our world. I pray that we come on one accord. Help us to look past our differences and see what we have in common. Help us to live a life of love, peace, understanding and unity. Help us be better examples of you. Help us to stop hurting each other, help us to love each other. Father remove from us all hate, jealousy, and envy. Create in us a clean heart and renew the right spirit within us. Fill us with your compassion, kindness, patience, goodness, and love.

In Jesus Name, Amen
Safe in his arms
Journey to please God
It is well. It is well.

Today's Prayer

Thank you Father for another wonderful day. Father, I thank you for knowing and trusting your word. Thank you that your word does what it says it will do. Today Father I pray for those who do not know what your word says for their lives. I pray for those that don't know that you are a promise keeper. I pray for those that are struggling and don't know that you are a way maker, a provider. I pray for those that are lost and don't know that you can be their light in darkness, a leader if they follow you. Father touch their lives. Give them an experience with you so that they will want a relationship with you. Let them know who you are.

In Jesus Name, Amen
Safe in his arms
Journey to please God
It is well. It is well.

"The Lord is my shepherd, I lack nothing. He makes me lie down in green pastures, he leads me beside quiet waters, he refreshes my soul. He guides me along the right paths for his name's sake. Even though I walk through the darkest valley, I will fear no evil, for you are with me; your rod and your staff, they comfort me. You prepare a table before me in the presence of my enemies. You anoint my head with oil, my cup overflows. Surely your goodness and love will follow me all the days of my life, and I will dwell in the house of the Lord forever." Psalms 23:1-6 NIV

Today's Prayer

Thank you, Father, for another wonderful day. No matter what comes our way today we will still give you glory, and we will still praise your name. I pray today for those that are feeling overwhelmed by their life circumstances. I pray God that they know you and they know that they can cast all of their cares on you. There is nothing too hard for you Father. There is nothing you can't overcome. You Father are always victorious. I pray Father that those that are overwhelmed, feeling defeated turn to you, cry out to you and you will rescue them. You will save them. You will provide for them. Thank you, Father, that you have already provided a way of escape for them.

In Jesus Name, Amen
Safe in his arms
Journey to please God
It is well. It is well.

"Some wandered in desert wastelands, finding no way to a city where they could settle. They were hungry and thirsty, and their lives ebbed away. Then they cried out to the Lord in their trouble, and he delivered them from their distress. He led them by a straight way to a city where they could settle. Let them give thanks to the Lord for his unfailing love and his wonderful deeds for mankind, for he satisfies the thirsty and fills the hungry with good things. Some sat in darkness, in utter darkness, prisoners suffering in iron chains, because they rebelled against God's commands and despised the plans of the Most High. So, he subjected them to bitter labor; they stumbled, and there was no one to help. Then they cried to the Lord in their trouble, and he saved them from their distress. He brought them out of darkness, the utter darkness, and broke away their chains. Let them give thanks to the Lord for his unfailing love and his wonderful deeds for mankind, for he breaks down gates of bronze and cuts through bars of iron. Some became fools through their rebellious ways and suffered affliction because of their iniquities. They loathed all food and drew near the gates of death. Then they cried to the Lord in their trouble, and he saved them from their distress. He sent out his word and healed them; he rescued them from the grave." Psalms 107:4-20 NIV

Today's Prayer

Thank you Father for another wonderful day. Father, I thank you for knowing and trusting your word. Thank you that your word does what it says it will do. Today Father I pray for those who do not know what your word says for their lives. I pray for those that don't know that you are a promise keeper. I pray for those that are struggling and don't know that you are a waymaker, a provider. I pray for those that are lost and don't know that you can be their light in darkness, a leader if they follow you. Father touch their lives. Give them an experience with you so that they will want a relationship with you. Let them know who you are.

In Jesus Name, Amen
Safe in his arms
Journey to please God
It is well. It is well.

"The Lord is my shepherd, I lack nothing. He makes me lie down in green pastures, he leads me beside quiet waters, he refreshes my soul. He guides me along the right paths for his name's sake. Even though I walk through the darkest valley, I will fear no evil, for you are with me; your rod and your staff, they comfort me. You prepare a table before me in the presence of my enemies. You anoint my head with oil; my cup overflows. Surely your goodness and love will follow me all the days of my life, and I will dwell in the house of the Lord forever." Psalms 23:1-6 NIV

Today's Prayer

Thank you, Father, for another wonderful day. Thank you for keeping and protecting us through our rest. Today Father I pray for peace of mind, and peace among each other. Father, your word says you will give perfect peace to those whose mind is stayed on you. Thank you, Father, for your perfect peace. Help us to focus on you Father. Help us to live in peace with ourselves and with each other. Thank you, Father, for your peace that surpasses all understanding. Through all that we go through, your word says that your peace will guard our hearts and our minds. Thank you, Father. Help us Father stay inside your peace.

In Jesus Name, Amen
Safe in his arms
Journey to please God
It is well. It is well.

"Now may the Lord of peace himself give you peace at all times and in every way. The Lord be with all of you."
2 Thessalonians 3:16 NIV

Today's Prayer

Thank you Father for another awesome day. Again I rise.
Because of you Father I rise to the obstacles I shall
overcome, and to the victories with my name on them.
Today Father I pray that you touch those that have
difficulties in their lives that they feel they can't overcome. I
pray for those that don't see how they are going to make it.
Let them know that with you they can do all things, That
with you, victory is theirs and that with you they are
overcomers. Show them Father that you are a provider, a
way maker. Remind them father that there is nothing too
hard for you. Lift their heads and give them the strength to
keep pushing. Rise up in them father. Rise up in their
situation.

In Jesus Name, Amen
Safe in his arms
Journey to please God
It is well. It is well.

Today's Prayer

Thank you Father for another wonderful day. Thank you for joy and happiness. Thank you Father that things don't always go how I want them to but they always work out for my good. Help me Father to see the good in everything and everyone. Today I pray Father that we would come on one accord, that our actions would be to please you. Father Line up our lives with your plans for us. Your plans are to help us, prosper us, give us hope and a future, not to hurt or harm us. Thank you Father for your plans for my life.

In Jesus Name, Amen
Safe in his arms
Journey to please God
It is well. It is well.

Today's Prayer

Thank you Father for another wonderful day. Thank you for love and forgiveness. Thank you for understanding and patience. Today Father, I thank you for your word says that we have all sinned and fallen short of your glory but you Father forgive and still love us in spite of our falls and our sins. Help us Father to have that same mindset as you when it comes to our brothers and sisters. Let us love in spite of. Let us forgive in spite of. Let us have patience and understanding in spite of.

In Jesus Name, Amen
Safe in his arms
Journey to please God
It is well. It is well.

.

Today's Prayer

Thank you Father for another wonderful day. Thank you for your peace that surrounds us on today. No matter what we encounter on today , whether it be good or bad, Father, you knew it was going to happen and you have already worked it for your glory. In other words whatever happens today we will be victorious. Today Father I pray for all elected officials. I pray that their mind is the same mind as the mind that is in Christ Jesus. I pray that you touch them daily creating a clean heart and renewing a right spirit within them. I pray Father that they know and hear your voice when they make choices, decisions that affect your children.

In Jesus Name, Amen
Safe in his arms
Journey to please God
It is well. It is well.

Today's Prayer

Thank you Father for another day. Thank you for the new mercies that come with this day. Thank you for dreams coming true, hearts being mended, and souls being saved. Today Father I pray for those that have lost hope, faith in you because of what they see and feel. I pray for those that are hopeless because of their current situation and all that is happening around them. I pray Father that you will revive them. Remind them Father that it is you that has been keeping them, it is you that has been providing ways out of no way, it is you Father that has been keeping them alive, it is you that has been fighting for them. Bring back to their remembrance the times you covered them from hurt harm and danger, the times when you moved stumbling blocks, hindrances out of their way. Remind them Father that if they call on you, you will answer like you did before. Show yourself mighty in their lives Father. Restore them Father. In Jesus Name, Amen

Safe in his arms
Journey to please God
It is well. It is well.

Today's Prayer

Thank you Father for another wonderful day. Thank you for all you have planned for this day. Help me to walk in your plan for me on today. Today Father I thank you for all the wonders you perform. I thank you for fighting for me. I thank you Father that you fight against seen and unseen dangers that come against me. You protect me when I don't even know I need protection. Thank you Father Thank you. Today Father I pray for our land. I pray you and not things become our focus. I pray our choices and actions line up with you and your word, plan for our lives. Don't let us be stiff necked people.

In Jesus Name, Amen
Safe in his arms
Journey to please God
It is well. It is well.

Today's Prayer

Thank you Father for another day.
Whew life can sometimes wear you thin. It can be
challenging and exciting. Father, I thank you that you have
built me to withstand the rain and the sunshine. Today Father
I pray strength for those that are experiencing rain, cloudy
days in their lives. I pray your direction and guidance for
them. I pray Father that they know you have not left them. I
pray as they are going through they know you are the one
carrying them through. Spread your arms of protection over
and around them so they won't quit, they won't give up.
Help them hold on until their morning of joy comes.

In Jesus Name, Amen
Safe in his arms
Journey to please God
It is well. It is well.

Today's Prayer

Thank you Father for another wonderful day. Thank you for divine protection as I slept. Thank you for covering my home and my family. Thank you for being able to wake and go about my daily task. Thank you Father for having everything needed to be victorious on today. Help me to Keep my mind, my actions, pleasing to you. Keep reminding and showing me Father that I can do all things through you. Don't let me get discouraged by what I see and hear around me.

In Jesus Name, Amen
Safe in his arms
Journey to please God
It is well. It is well.

Today's Prayer

Thank you Father for another day. Thank you Father that I am here, present, in my right mind, able to walk, talk, move around, work, come and go as I see fit. Thank you Father for that is more than enough to praise you. There are some who can't do those things. As I look around my life, feeling sorry for myself, wondering why, and wishing things were different, shouldn't be a part of what I do. Through everything I have gone through Father you kept me. Not just the good but everything, you have provided a way, and covered me. The least I can do is be grateful and not complain. Thank you Father for continuously and consistently showing your love for me. Forgive me for the times I seem ungrateful for all that you do. I am Redirecting my focus, my attention on the good and not the bad; what I have and not what I want. Grateful. Thankful.

In Jesus Name, Amen
Safe in his arms
Journey to please God
It is well. It is well.

Today's Prayer

Thank you Father for another day. Thank you for new mercies and new Blessings. Thank you for sweet rest and early rising. As I go through my day I thank you for protection from seen and unseen dangers. I ask that you Help me to walk in your way and your will. Help me Father to be pleasing and acceptable to you. Help me to handle whatever comes my way the way you would handle it. On today Father I cast all my cares on you. I lean on you and I thank you that all will go according to how you have predestined it to go.

In Jesus Name, Amen
Safe in his arms
Journey to please God
It is well. It is well.

Today's Prayer

Thank you Father for another fantastic day. Thank you for being my God and knowing me inside out. Thank you for knowing what I need and what I don't; for your strength when I am weak, and hope when I am feeling hopeless. Thank you Father that in due season I shall reap a harvest if I Faint not. Help me to not faint Father. Help me to hold on. Help me to keep going. Help me stay focused on you Father. Help me Father to stay in your will. Don't give up, keep going. Joy will come. Victory will come. Peace will come. In Jesus Name, Amen

Safe in his arms
Journey to please God
It is well. It is well.

Today's Prayer

Thank you Father for another wonderful day. Thank you for the new mercies that come with the new day. Thank you Father that no matter how much or how long the rain falls the sun always shines afterwards. Thank you for learning to be patient through and thankful for the rain. Thank you Father that the rain washes away the excess debris that comes to hinder or distract me. Thank you father that sometimes the rain is fertilizer for my growth to help me blossom. I'm just thankful that whatever the purpose, you Father are there with me, leading, and guiding me through.

In Jesus Name, Amen
Safe in his arms
Journey to please God
It is well. It is well.

Today's Prayer

Thank you Father for another wonderful day and opportunity to glorify you, to praise you, to thank you, and to lift up your name. Mercy Father you are awesome, you are good, you are merciful, you are forgiving, you are loving, you are a healer, deliver, provider, protector, comforter. Father you are... I thank you for accepting me as I am, loving me as I am, working with me to become what you created me to be and most of all loving me regardless of my shortcomings. I am just grateful, thankful for having you Father in my life for you Father thinking enough of me to call me daughter, child, friend.

In Jesus Name, Amen
Safe in his arms
Journey to please God
It is well. It is well.

Today's Prayer

Thank you Father for another awesome day. Thank you Father that not only do you hear our prayers but you answer them as well. Thank you for knowing what we need, when we need it and most of all thank you for being a supplier of those needs. Lord your grace and mercy goes beyond what I can imagine. I am just so grateful that you withhold nothing good from me. Your blessings are unmeasurable and I am grateful that you see me as deserving of your blessings. Thank you Father. Thank you.

In Jesus Name, Amen
Safe in his arms
Journey to please God
It is well. It is well.

Today's Prayer

Thank you Father for another wonderful day. Thank you for your grace and your mercy. Thank you for the blood of Jesus that covers, keeps and protects me. Thank you Father for going before me and preparing the way for me. Help me Father to stay on your path, walk in your way. Help me to keep my mind on you and your will. Forgive me for the times I do /did stray. Thank you for not holding those times against me. Thank you that you are a God of many chances. In Jesus Name, Amen

Safe in his arms
Journey to please God
It is well. It is well.

Today's Prayer

Thank you Father for another day. Thank you for your
protection through seen and unseen dangers. Thank you for
your protection from me and my wants that don't line up
with your will for my life. Thank you for knowing who I am
and having plans for me. Thank you for your plans are for
my good and for your working all, everything for that good
to manifest.

In Jesus Name, Amen
Safe in his arms
Journey to please God
It is well. It is well.

Today's Prayer

Thank you Father for another day.
Thank you for allowing me to have rest and early rising this morning. Thank you Father that you are and all knowing, all seeing God. Thank you for being a prayer answering God, a healer, a deliverer, a protector, a provider. Thank you for being everything I need. Thank you for being God. Help me not to get distracted by what I see and feel. Help me father to look to and lean on you.

In Jesus Name, Amen
Safe in his arms
Journey to please God
It is well. It is well.

Today's Prayer

Thank you Father for another day. Thank you that I'm up and ready to face another day. Thank you for this is the day you have made and I am rejoicing in it. Thank you that you already knew this day would happen and that you have given me all that I need to make it through the day. Help me to walk/ act in your peace, your joy, your strength, and your power.

In Jesus Name, Amen
Safe in his arms
Journey to please God
It is well. It is well.

Today's Prayer

Thank you Father for another day. I just want to thank you Father for all that you are doing for me. You let me rise each morning in my right mind. Father I thank you because if it wasn't for you I don't know how I would be, where I would be, or what I would be like. Lord, I thank you. Father I Thank you. Father, I thank you that you haven't turned your back on me, you haven't walked away from me, you haven't left me alone. Help me Father to stay in your will, on your path. I am so undeserving and yet you remain faithful to me. Each day you give me new mercies, another chance. Thank you Father. Thank you.

In Jesus name, Amen
Safe in his arms
Journey to please God
It is well. It is well.

Today's Prayer

Thank you Father for another day. Thank you for loving me enough to wake me in my right mind, for allowing me the ability to walk, talk, move around without the aid of others. Even in my down, not so good days you are still with me; watching over me, protecting, me, encouraging me, leading, guiding me, and strengthening me. Thank you Father. Thank you. Help me not to walk, move, step, or talk myself outside of your will, your covering.

In Jesus Name, Amen
Safe in his arms
Journey to please God
It is well. It is well.

Today's Prayer

Thank you Father for another day. Thank you that when I don't understand, I can rely on you to show me the way, to make it clear. Thank you Father that when things get difficult you are there, and I can cast my burdens on you. Thank you Father for your peace and strength. Not by my power but by your power Father. Thank you Father for your power.

In Jesus Name, Amen
Safe in his arms
Journey to please God
It is well. It is well.

Today's Prayer

Thank you Father for another day. Thank you that when I don't understand, I can rely on you to show me the way, to make it clear. Thank you Father that when things get difficult you are there, and I can cast my burdens on you. Thank you Father for your peace and strength. Not by my power but by your power Father. Thank you Father for your power.
In Jesus Name, Amen

Safe in his arms
Journey to please God
It is well. It is well.

Today's Prayer

Thank you Father for another day. Thank you Father for not just knowing you but for having a relationship with you as well. Thank you that I am your child. Thank you that when it feels like I am walking through the shadows of death you are still with me; leading, guiding and protecting me. Thank you Father for your righteousness and faithfulness to me. Thank you for hearing me when I call you and making my pathways straight. Thank you Father for just loving me.

In Jesus name, Amen
Safe in his arms
Journey to please God
It is well. It is well.

Today's Prayer

Thank you Father for another day. Thank you for keeping and strengthening me. Thank you for being God. Thank you for leading, guiding, and directing my life. Thank you for your peace. Help me to live in your peace.

In Jesus Name, Amen
Safe in his arms
Journey to please God

Prophetess Angie Smith

Prophetess Smith is the Founder and President of *Grace's Haven,* a nonprofit that was created to share the word of God. The mission of Grace's Haven of SC to offer resources and services to enhance the lives of economically challenged women and families throughout South Carolina in particular rural communities. Grace's Haven's Motto is "We are making a difference in our communities one service at time" which is in line with Prophetess Smith's belief that we are all servants of God. We are here to serve others. We will be rewarded for what we do to make the lives of those we come in contact with better.

Prophetess Smith received her Bachelors in Journalism from Benedict College and her Masters in Community Services from Ashford University. She is a member of Gaston Community Church of Praise in Gaston SC under the leadership of Pastor Talmadge Dixon. Prophetess Smith attended New Life Bible College under the Leadership of Bishop Cardell Sutton and Dr. Carolyn Sutton.

She currently resides in West Columbia SC with her teen daughter Grace Smith. She was married to the late Alexander Smith. She is the daughter of Geraldine and the late Herman Grant. She has one sister Gwen Williams and one brother the late Michael Grant.

Prophetess Angie Smith's favorite scriptures are: *"I have the strength to face all conditions by the power that Christ gives me."* Philippians 4:13 GNB and "Moses answered, *"Don't be afraid! Stand your ground, and you will see what the LORD will do to save you today; you will never see these Egyptians again. The LORD will fight for you, and there is no need for you to do anything."* Exodus 14:13-14 GNB

Lightning Source UK Ltd.
Milton Keynes UK
UKHW050653280521
384527UK00003B/11